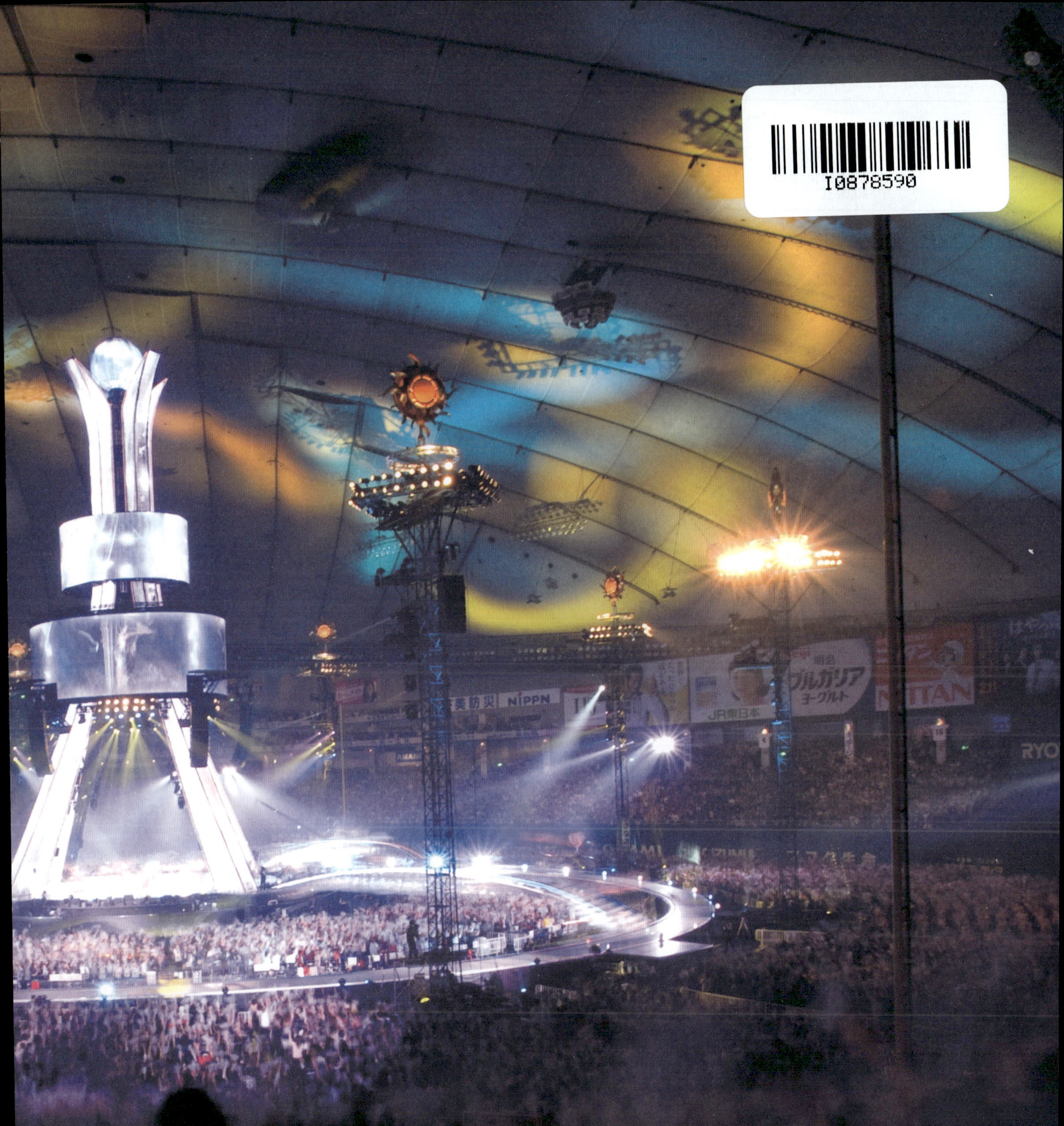
NIPPN
JR東日本
明治
ブルガリア
ヨーグルト
NITTAN

Hiro in Exile
The Creation of a J-Pop Empire

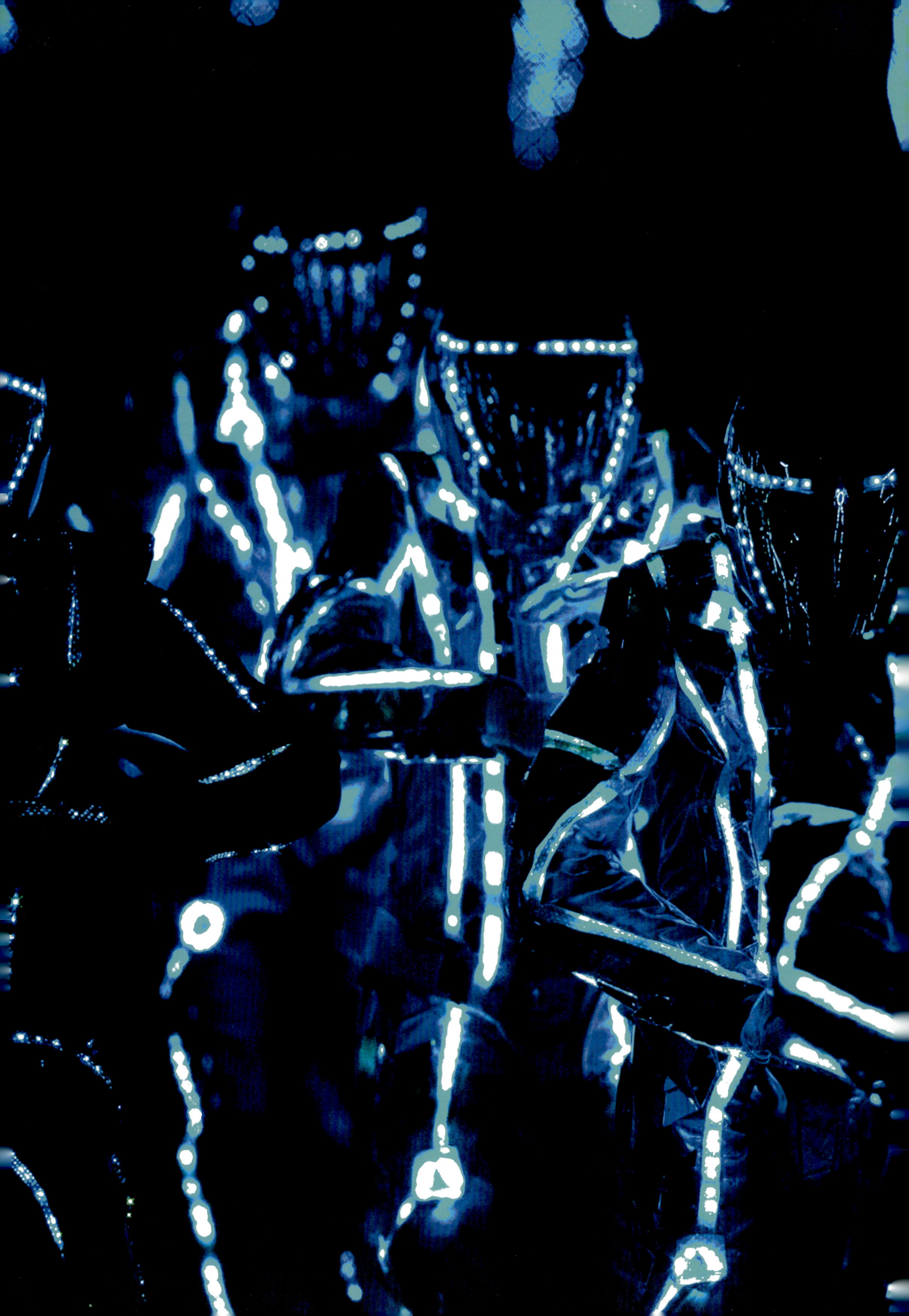

Friday, July 19
1:55 p.m.
125

5017

J-Soul Brother

A Conversation with Hiro and Verbal August 15, 2017

I.
I was young, and I just thought it was cool.

VERBAL: What was your first encounter with dance?

HIRO: I had always loved music since I was a child. In middle school, back when I lived in Yokohama, I frequently watched "Billboard TV," a TV show broadcasted on TV Kanagawa, which played music videos of western hit songs. This show sparked my interest in dance and dance music by introducing me to artists like Michael Jackson. At the age of 15, I would frequently be at discos, and before I knew it I was heavily into dance. There were no dance schools back then, so I learned mainly through nightlife, but I consciously aspired to be a dancer for the first time at the age of 19 when New Jack Swing became the trend.

VERBAL: Which artist did you look up to at that time?

HIRO: I looked up to New Jack Swing artists, especially New Edition, Guy, and of course, Bobby Brown. When I visited Los Angeles at the age of 19 I delved more and more deeply into music and dance culture. I then visited New York, where I first heard "real" Hip-Hop. The music, fashion and the culture immediately grabbed my heart, and that basically sums up my entire 20's.

VERBAL: There was actually a time when I aspired to be a dancer myself, just to get girls (laughs), but I was struck when I first saw you and your group ZOO perform on TV. I didn't know Japanese people could dance with such style and attitude. Back then I was just a fan, but you being someone who was at the forefront of the club and dance scene, how was the street culture and fashion at that time period?

HIRO: My group ZOO originally evolved from a dance group called LMD, which was founded through an audition program aired on TV Asahi called "DADA LMD". This was back in 1990, when everyday was a party. Clubs and discos throughout Yokohama, Roppongi, Shinjuku were packed every single night. The internet did not exist and information was not available for everyone, so the amount of new information you had mattered a lot. I would integrate and express fashion and music that was popular in LA and New York into my style as fast as I could. I wore dreads when nobody

p.18–20: HIRO in New York City, 2013. Photography by Kei Ogata

Opposite page:
A few of over 150 MTV Japan awards that EXILE and associated acts have received in the last seventeen years.
Photography by Kei Ogata

else did, as a way of expressing myself. I was young, and I just thought it was cool. Today information is equally available and everything is clean and concise, while back then it was more chaotic which created a unique kind of excitement. I feel we will never see such an era again.

VERBAL: I agree, that was a unique, chaotic time period. Actually, this was when I first met you. I was waiting for a friend at the game arcade on the first floor of Roppongi Square Building, where all the clubs were, when you coincidentally walked out of the elevator. I got so excited I was like, "I've seen him on TV!" (laughs).

HIRO: Back then, information was only available in the streets. Even in New York and Los Angeles, I was able to meet people and directly be involved in the music, fashion and culture only because I was physically there.

VERBAL: The early 1990s seemed like a rough time for New York.

HIRO: Yes, my first trips were before Giuliani became mayor so it was very rough, and since the areas I frequented were considered even by New Yorkers at the time as "high-crime" areas, I felt a type of fear that I had never experienced. It must be hard to imagine because the people in New York are so friendly today.

VERBAL: I agree. I've actually heard that the new "cool" is to be kind to people, while back then being "bad" or "rude" was considered to be "cool".

HIRO: That is such a better trend! (laughs). But seriously, Hip-Hop was already a huge part of me before I left for New York, but meeting the people who created this culture, in the neighborhoods where they lived, to witness their energy and their love for life despite very trying circumstances, was truly inspiring and enlightening.

II.
I started to focus on the meaning of entertainment.

VERBAL: When did your career as a dancer start?

HIRO: After ZOO was founded.

VERBAL: You mentioned this before, but can you take us back to when ZOO took off?

HIRO: When I performed on an audition program called "DADA LMD", I was invited to be part of a dance team that the program was trying to create, called LMD. At that time I was working at a club in Roppongi called "Circus," and was motivated to become the owner, so I was not too interested in the offer. However,

MUSIC TELEVISION
Best Choreography Award
EXILE
Best Pop Video

I soon realized that dancing on TV as part of LMD was fun, got me popular with girls, and that it was not such a bad job after all. When our group's name changed to ZOO, I did not have many opinions about it, other than the fact that I thought it was a weird name (laughs). I was young and clueless. There was nobody around me who could teach me the rules and discipline of working in the industry, and I caused a lot of trouble with my childish behavior.

VERBAL: Back then dance and hip-hop was not established as "entertainment" to the mass, so a group like ZOO which infused dancers and singers was the first of its kind.

HIRO: We were not a dance team, nor a chorus group. The combination of dancers and singers was definitely something new in Japan. My experience, being the youngest member of a new, successful group, is still the foundation of my entire career. I say this in a lot of interviews, but I have always felt that dancers need vocalists as avatars who express their feelings through words. To me, the combination of dancers and vocalists was inevitable.

VERBAL: When did you start having a producer's mindset?

HIRO: The disbanding of ZOO made me realize how young and selfish I was. As I gained more experience in the industry, my mindset also started to change. When I was a backup dancer for the group Dreams Come True, we would have discussions during rehearsals on what we can do to make the fans happy. Embarrassingly enough, I had never thought about that in my entire career, and I still remember these discussions as if they happened yesterday. It was around this time that I started to focus on the meaning of entertainment.

VERBAL: I have always known you to be hands-on from start to the end, when it comes to music and stage production. A couple days ago when I attended the meeting on J Soul Brothers III's upcoming tour with you, and I noticed that you have the ability to motivate the artists and make them focus on entertaining the fans at the same time. How do you do that?

HIRO: In the end, no matter how pleased we are, there is no subsequent endeavor if the fans are not happy. Focusing on short-term benefits prevents us from looking at the big picture and the value of the brand. Since its founding, LDH has given its all to every show with the sole purpose of making the fans happy. It may sound cheesy, but it's true. I also constantly communicate with the artists, and we know each other's personalities very well, so the trust we have is very special.

III.
Creating something only has true meaning when it is done with somebody who shares the same spirit

VERBAL: Your means of building a relationship with people is something that has inspired me a lot. For example, when you are interested in an artist, you immediately try to meet him/her in person. Where does that desire to immediately make a personal connection come from?

HIRO: In the end, it's all about the person. LDH owes its success to the people I've been able to meet in my life. Creating something only has true meaning when it is done with somebody who shares the same spirit, and meeting them in person is the only way to find out. LDH has always treasured this spirit, and a great example is when we built our second EXPG (dance school) in Miyazaki. From a business point of view, a metropolitan city such as Nagoya or Osaka should have been chosen as the next EXPG location following Tokyo. However, we chose to work with a close friend who had been running a dance school in Miyazaki as our next location. LDH Kitchen, our restaurant branch, was also founded with a classmate who was pursuing his career as a chef, to create restaurants where our artists can casually dine.

VERBAL: Are a lot of LDH employees are your childhood friends as well?

HIRO: Yes, and we often receive negative opinions on this. However, LDH started with less than 10 people, and up until today we have experienced so many failures. There's a special trust that I share with my childhood friends, and it makes it easier for us to share the same vision. Of course, after changing our corporate structure in 2017 and as we focus on overseas expansion, we expect to welcome a lot of new teammates.

VERBAL: There is a question I have always wanted to ask you. Most foreign management companies outsource everything : for example, even Scooter Braun, who manages Justin Bieber, runs his company with less than 30 employees. What is LDH's intention in doing everything in-house?

HIRO: I strongly believe in teamwork, or the Japanese term "wa." I believe that a successful artist owes that success not only to his own talent, but more importantly to the teamwork of everybody involved. There are many obvious benefits to outsourcing, but the freedom to create anything allows us to fully inject the spirit of bringing happiness to the fans. It also motivates the employees, and even if something fails, they owe it to themselves. The teamwork of the staff and the artists is the foundation of LDH. Although I believe this is a very Japanese way of thinking, I also know that a lot of foreign management companies are interested in our business model.

Following spread: HIRO in the main conference room of the LDH headquarters in Meguro-ku, Tokyo, 2015. Photography by Kei Ogata

p.28–31: HIRO in New York City, 2013. Photography by Kei Ogata

VERBAL: Speaking of overseas, LDH is putting a lot of work into expanding into Asia, U.S.A., and Europe.

HIRO: You, VERBAL, have always been on the forefront of our overseas projects, and have already done so much for LDH. You are well respected in both music and fashion worlds, and have strong connections with foreign artists. You are constantly moving around, but very respectful and polite. I am inspired by your energy every time we have a conversation. You're a genius when it comes to thinking of new ideas based off of your past experiences.

VERBAL: Your words are too kind, but thank you (laughs). Your vision of overseas expansion is something that has never existed in the Japanese entertainment industry. Most companies hesitate to try something new overseas, but you always support our ideas by saying "let's try it", even for the most difficult projects. When I entered my 30's there was a point in my life where I realized my creative energy was starting to fade, and I thought it was something inevitable. However, I got that passion back when I met you, and was inspired from your positive energy.

HIRO: Our base will always be in Japan, but the thought of challenging our abilities in the foreign market is simply exciting. Of course we will face a lot of difficulties, but the goal to collaborate with foreign artists or to do a show overseas leads to greater motivation for our artists, which leads to more vitality throughout the entire company. We are already witnessing a cycle of positive energy, and we are seeing a connection on how to do things in the Asian and the Western market while still staying focused on the Japanese market. I believe that the next 1~2 years will be very exciting for LDH.

VERBAL: Throughout your career you have done so much to help fulfill so many people's dreams. About what percent of your dreams have been fulfilled?

HIRO: I would say 60%, but if I include my dreams overseas, maybe about 40%. I am currently 48 years old, and my goal by 55 is to create an overall entertainment facility that incorporates everything LDH has to offer, from dome tours, theatres to apparel stores and restaurants. I want this place to attract tourists from all over the world. I would love for our challenges to bring more smiles on people's faces. When I was a performer of EXILE, I was able to absorb positive energy directly from the fans. After stepping down to focus on the creative side of things, that opportunity has decreased, and I have had to face the "raw" side of the industry many times. This has made me further realize my responsibility to embody and to deliver Love, Dream and Happiness. I believe that creating an "LDH Land", a place like Disney Land or Universal Studios that brings happiness through entertainment, is the ultimate way of embodying this spirit. As we become more active overseas, it is also exciting to imagine what will happen in Asia, U.S.A, and Europe. This excitement reminds me of my first trip to the United States. After I fulfill every dream I just mentioned, I will finally be free to do whatever I want at the age of 60. I might even compose the most ludicrous song, and have a foreign superstar perform it (laughs).

The Dancer

Tribes

"EXILE TRIBE is a place where talented artists come together to collaborate with each other, find out how to maximize their entertainment potential, and make those goals into reality. At EXILE TRIBE, entertainment without limits is the name of the game. The EXILE TRIBE brand has since expanded into live venues and fashion outlets, creating new opportunities for artists to express their craft and perform at all kinds of events. All of this will lead to a constant stream of new and exciting entertainment. Because, in the end, our goal is to create entertainment that can put smiles on the faces of people around the world."
— HIRO

EXILE

J Soul Brothers formed in 1999 under HIRO's leadership and was renamed EXILE in 2001. Original members included HIRO, MATSU (Toshio Matsumoto), ÜSA, MAKIDAI, SHUN, and ATSUSHI.

SHUN left the group to pursue a solo career in 2006. In June the same year, AKIRA joined as a performer. Later that year, EXILE held a competition entitled [EXILE Vocal Battle Audition 2006 ~ASIAN DREAM~] to find a new vocalist. Among the 10,000 competitors, TAKAHIRO emerged as the winner, and EXILE's second chapter began.

In 2009, J Soul Brothers II members Kenchi Tachibana, Keiji Kuroki, TETSUYA, NESMITH, SHOKICHI, NAOTO, and Naoki Kobayashi joined EXILE, announcing the group's third chapter.

That year, EXILE created and donated the track "Taiyo no Kuni" to celebrate the twentieth anniversary of the accession to the throne of the present emperor.

In 2013, HIRO stepped down from his role as performer, and focused his energies on growing LDH full-time. LDH, which stands for love, dream and happiness, is the parent company of EXILE which Hiro also founded.

In 2014, EXILE held [EXILE PERFORMER BATTLE AUDITION] and welcomed 5 new performers to the group (Takanori Iwata, Alan Shirahama, Mandy Sekiguchi, Sekai, and Taiki Sato). This marked the beginning of EXILE's fourth chapter.

In 2015, original members MATSU, ÜSA, and MAKIDAI retired from the positions as performers in the group.

Currently, EXILE has grown into a 19-member dance and vocal group that includes EXILE HIRO, Toshio Matsumoto, EXILE ÜSA, EXILE MAKIDAI, EXILE ATSUSHI, EXILE TAKAHIRO, Kenchi Tachibana, Keiji Kuroki, EXILE TETSUYA, EXILE NESMITH, EXILE SHOKICHI, EXILE NAOTO, Naoki Kobayashi, Takanori Iwata, Alan Shirahama, Mandy Sekiguchi, Sekai, and Taiki Sato.

EXILE TRIBE

(See pages 40–41) Used as the title for a 2012 tour, EXILE TRIBE represented just that, a unified and tribal sensibility, and an organizing principle for EXILE and its associated acts.

It was HIRO's intention that the members of the tribe all share the same EXILE spirit, one embodied in the three words behind the

Opposite page: EXILE, 2014
Top row, left to right: Taiki Sato, Alan Shirahama, Mandy Sekiguchi, Takanori Iwata, and Sekai;
Middle row, left to right: Naoki Kobayashi, Keiji Kuroki, EXILE TETSUYA, EXILE SHOKICHI, EXILE NAOTO, EXILE NESMITH, and Kenchi Tachibana;
Bottom row, left to right: EXILE AKIRA, Toshio Matsumoto, EXILE TAKAHIRO, EXILE HIRO, EXILE ATSUSHI, EXILE ÜSA, and EXILE MAKIDAI

acronym LDH: love, dream and happiness, as well as the same motivation in creating meaningful entertainment.

In addition to EXILE, the 2012 tour featured performances from groups & individual artists, such as EXILE ATSUSHI, J Soul Brothers II (now known as EXILE THE SECOND), J Soul Brothers III, DANCE EARTH PARTY, DJ MAKIDAI, MATSU BOCCHI (Toshio Matsumoto's solo project), E-girls, and GENERATIONS.

In September 2012, EXILE TRIBE released their first single; a collaboration between EXILE and J Soul Brothers III titled "24karats TRIBE OF GOLD".

For the second single, J Soul Brothers III and GENERATIONS collaborated on the track "BURNIN' UP." Since then, EXILE TRIBE has continued to perform and release tracks with various artists.

EXILE TRIBE released its third single, titled "THE REVOLUTION" in 2014. Later the same year, the album *EXILE TRIBE REVOLUTION* was released. During the *EXILE TRIBE PERFECT YEAR 2014* tour, 13 EXILE TRIBE projects performed across Japan in front of a total of 2 million fans. Afterwards, artists including THE RAMPAGE from EXILE TRIBE, GEKIDAN EXILE (a theatrical troupe consisting of professional actors and EXILE members, see page 159), and SAMURIZE from EXILE TRIBE (an LED performance group, see pages 12–13 and 95) also took on the EXILE TRIBE name.

EXILE THE SECOND

(See pages 44–45) The group, THE SECOND from EXILE, was announced in July 2012. They released their first single in November of the same year.

In May 2016, the group was renamed to EXILE THE SECOND. Current members include Kenchi Tachibana, Keiji Kuroki, EXILE TETSUYA, EXILE NESMITH, EXILE SHOKICHI, and EXILE AKIRA.

J Soul Brothers III from EXILE TRIBE

(See pages 46–47) A dance and vocal group that continues the EXILE legacy.

Performers include group leader EXILE NAOTO, Naoki Kobayashi, ELLY, Kenjiro Yamashita, and Takanori Iwata, a new EXILE member. Vocals are handled by winners of [EXILE Presents VOCAL BATTLE AUDITION 2], Ryuji Imaichi and Hiroomi Tosaka. J Soul Brothers III made their major debut in November 2010 with their single "Best Friend's Girl."

GENERATIONS from EXILE TRIBE

(See pages 48–49) GENERATIONS from EXILE TRIBE is a dance-vocal group born from EXILE TRIBE. Fusing together a uniquely Japanese personality with international attitude, GENERATIONS consists of seven members, two vocalists and five performers. The group carries on EXILE's DNA through EXILE-powered events and mentorship. The two vocalists, Ryota Katayose and Ryuto Kazuhara, were discovered after their standout performances

Above:
EXILE, 2015
Left to right:
Kenchi Tachibana, EXILE AKIRA, EXILE NESMITH, Alan Shirahama, EXILE ÜSA, Mandy Sekiguchi, Toshio Matsumoto, Sekai, EXILE ATSUSHI, EXILE HIRO, EXILE TAKAHIRO, EXILE MAKIDAI, Taiki Sato, EXILE TETSUYA, Naoki Kobayashi, EXILE SHOKICHI, EXILE NAOTO, Takanori Iwata, and Keiji Kuroki

during [EXILE presents VOCAL BATTLE AUDITION 2] and were chosen from over 30,000 contestants to record with and join the EXILE family. The five performers, Alan Shirahama, Reo Sano, Hayato Komori, Mandy Sekiguchi, and Yuta Nakatsuka, were handpicked from EXPG (EXILE PROFESSIONAL GYM) where they perfected their dance talents from a young age and form the backbone of GENERATIONS today.

Formed in 2012, GENERATIONS has seen remarkable success domestically both critically and commercially. Their self-titled debut album, released in 2013, reached #1 on the Oricon Weekly Album Chart. The group followed their debut with sold out live shows across Japan. Their latest album "SPEEDSTER" brought them their 3rd consecutive #1 hit on the Oricon Weekly Album Chart, and led to an even more successful touring schedule including a 2017 tour that saw GENERATIONS perform in New York, Los Angeles, Taipei & Macau.

PKCZ®

(See pages 50-51) EXILE HIRO, DJ MAKIDAI (EXILE), VERBAL (from m-flo, TERIYAKI BOYZ, HONEST BOYZ®, and AMBUSH®), and DJ DARUMA are the core members of PKCZ®, a creative team bringing new value to the Japanese music and fashion scene. With "MIX the WORLD" as their slogan, PKCZ® has collaborated with various artists from domestic talent to global stars such as Afrojack and Snoop Dogg.

After producing Japan's biggest Halloween party titled "ELECTRIC HALLOWEEN" with over 20,000 attendees, PKCZ® went on to open their first store/gallery space, PKCZ® GALLERY STORE in 2015, that features fashion inspired by group members. PKCZ® released their first single "PLAY THAT feat. HIROOMI TOSAKA, Crystal Kay, CRAZYBOY" on April 28, 2017. This single dominated the Japanese pop charts. In June 2017, they kicked off the summer with a performance at ULTRA MUSIC FESTIVAL SINGAPORE, and TOMORROWLAND 2017.

HONEST BOYZ®

(See pages 52-53) HONEST BOYZ consists of NIGO®, EXILE NAOTO, VERBAL (PKCZ®), SWAY(DOBERMAN INFINITY), and MANDY (from GENERATIONS). They debuted to the public in April 2016 with a soundtrack for a TV Drama series on TV Tokyo, *Night Hero Naoto*, starring EXILE NAOTO himself.

THE RAMPAGE from EXILE TRIBE

(See pages 54-55) Rooted in hip-hop culture, this 16-member dance and vocal group was formed by bringing together talent found through three different public auditions; 2014's [EXILE PERFORMER BATTLE AUDITION], which added a new EXILE member, the vocalist-centered [VOCAL BATTLE AUDITION 4], and the internationally focused [GLOBAL JAPAN CHALLENGE]. Sixteen of the best young vocalists and performers were brought together to form THE RAMPAGE from EXILE TRIBE.

In the intervening years since the group was formed, they honed their skills as performers by learning from the best during two different EXILE TRIBE national tours, finally making their major debut in January 2017. As the name of the group implies, THE RAMPAGE from EXILE TRIBE hits the stage with their own aggressive brand of hip-hop-flavored entertainment.

FANTASTICS

(See pages 56–57) A 7-member performance group that features EXILE members Sekai and Taiki Sato as leaders, and five specially chosen performers from EXILE GENERATIONS (a group made up from members of the dance, vocal, and performance school EXILE PROFESSIONAL GYM).

E.G. Family

In April 2011, the groups Dream, Happiness, and Flower (see pages 60–61 and 64–67) got together to form E-girls and initiate the "girls' entertainment project" within LDH.

In the six years since their forming, the members of E-girls continued to discuss and share their ideas about the group and its future, and they decided that the best way to keep E-girls exciting and relevant was to form a new group focused on each member's individual abilities. E-girls evolved into E.G. Family, a largely woman-centric and woman-led entertainment project within LDH that drew from the EXILE TRIBE model. The E.G. Family currently consists of E-girls, Dream Ami, DANCE EARTH PARTY, Happiness, Flower, ShuuKaRen, and Sudannayuzuyully. The eleven original members retained the E-girls name, but at their core, the group's sensibility was brand new.

Using what they learned through their experiences within the constituent groups, the E.G Family continues to evolve as a place where members can realize their individual aspirations.

DANCE EARTH PARTY

(See pages 58–59) Making the world happy through dance.

That sentiment is what spurred EXILE ÜSA, one of the founding members of EXILE, on a journey to celebrate the origins and practice of dance in Japan and around the world. His quest began in 2006, traveling the globe to dance with locals, learning the dance traditions of a particular city or region. His extensive and immersive itinerary only serve to reinforce a deeply-held belief, that dance is a universal language that can overcome boundaries and words. EXILE ÜSA decided he wanted to use his experiences to give back to the community, and that is how the DANCE EARTH project came about.

The group DANCE EARTH PARTY has one mandate: to spread the DANCE EARTH philosophy through music. Since 2015, DANCE EARTH PARTY's official members include EXILE ÜSA, EXILE TETSUYA (performer), and Dream Shizuka (vocalist). To that end, the group is intimately linked with many of EXILE ÜSA's community outreach and charitable initiatives, spreading a message of "one world, one love."

Dream Aya

(See page 60) Dream Aya was previously a member of Dream, a precursor group formed in early 2011 whose members are at the core of E-girls (see pages 62–63). She announced on June 5, 2017 that she will focus on her new role as chief creative manager of E-girls.

Dream Ami

(See page 61) Dream Ami was also a former member of Dream.

With her single "Dress wo Nuida Cinderella" in 2015, she became the first member of E-girls to release a solo single. Besides her activity as a musical artist, she is making her name known around the entertainment industry as a TV MC and a radio personality. She announced on June 5, 2017 that she will focus more on her solo activities.

E-girls

(See pages 62–63) E-girls is a "girls' entertainment project" within LDH that inherited the EXILE DNA for excellence in dance-driven entertainment.

Following spread:
EXILE THE SECOND, 2017
Left to right:
Keiji Kuroki, EXILE AKIRA, EXILE SHOKICHI, EXILE TETSUYA, EXILE NESMITH, and Kenchi Tachibana

p.46–47:
J Soul Brothers III from EXILE TRIBE, 2017
Left to right:
Takanori Iwata, NAOTO, Hiroomi Tosaka, Naoki Kobayashi, Ryuji Imaichi, ELLY, and Kenjiro Yamashita

Above:
GENERATIONS from EXILE TRIBE, 2017
Left to right:
Yuta Nakatsuka, Alan Shirahama, Reo Sano, Ryuto Kazuhara, Ryota Katayose, Hayato Komori, and Mandy Sekiguchi

Since their debut in December 2011 with the single "Celebration!," E-girls have had as their focus presenting the best versions of themselves to the timing of their album and single releases, their song concepts, and their approach to live performance.

Rotating members around depending on the song allows for new and engaging combinations, creating modules that continually draw from and reinforce EXILE's core values and themes. Current members include SAYAKA, Kaede, Karen Fujii, YURINO, Anna Suda, Reina Washio, Nozomi Bando, Harumi Sato, Anna Ishii, Nonoka Yamaguchi, and Yuzuna Takebe.

Happiness

(See pages 64–65) Before their debut, Happiness was featured in EXILE's tours and music videos. They made their debut in Feburary of 2011 with the release of the single "Kiss Me." Members include SAYAKA, KAEDE, Karen Fujii, MIYUU, and YURINO. In June 2013, Anna Suda and Ruri Kawamoto joined the group, leading to a new chapter in the evo-

lution of Happiness. The group is also part of the E.G. family.

Flower

(See page 66–67) Formed in February of 2011 by the winners of *EXILE Presents VOCAL BATTLE AUDITION3 ~For Girls~*, an audition that brought in over 30,000 competitors.

The group debuted in October 2011 with the single "Still," a track that struck a chord with a younger female audience, helping it reach #5 on the Oricon chart.

From the outset, Flower has been a girls' group that focuses on the unique individuality of each member, as they also work as actresses and models in addition to their activities with the group.

Members include Shuuka Fujii, Manami Shigetome, Mio Nakajima, Reina Washio, Nozomi Bando, and Harumi Sato. The group, like Happiness is also a member of the E.G. family.

ShuuKaRen

(See page 68–69) A unit composed of two sisters

Following spread: PKCZ®, 2017
Left to right: DJ MAKIDAI, VERBAL, and DJ DARUMA

DIE YOUN

FILA

BUSH

p.52–53:
HONEST BOYZ®, 2016
Left to right:
VERBAL, MANDY, NAOTO, SWAY, and NIGO®

p.54–55:
THE RAMPAGE from EXILE TRIBE
Left to right:
Makoto Hasegawa, Shohei Urakawa, LIKIYA, Kaisei Takechi, Shogo Yamamoto, Kenta Kamiya, Hokuto Yoshino, Kazuma Kawamura, Itsuki Fujiwara, Zin, RIKU, Rui Yonamine, Ryu, Takuma Goto, Shogo Iwaya, and Takahide Suzuki

p.56–57:
FANTASTICS
Left to right:
Reiya Sekiguchi, Keito Kimura, Taiki Sato, Natsuki Sawamoto, Shota Nakao, Sekai, and Natsuki Hori

Previous spread:
DANCE EARTH PARTY
Left to right:
EXILE TETSUYA, Dream Shizuka, and EXILE ÜSA

from Osaka. They are both popular members of E-girls, with older sister Shuuka Fujii in Flower, and younger sister Karen Fujii in Happiness. They are also prominently featured in the fashion magazine *JJ* as exclusive models.

Their first "style book" *ANTITHESE*, was released in January 2016 and was a huge hit, going on to sell more than 100,000 copies. This proved their popularity as not only artists, but as models as well. On October 5, 2016, the Fujii sisters formed ShuuKaRen. For their first single "UNIVERSE," Shuuka, originally a performer, made her debut as a vocalist, with Karen as MC. ShuuKaRen is also part of the E.G. family.

Sudannayuzuyully

(See pages 70–71) E-girls and Happiness performer Anna Suda, YURINO, and E-girls member Yuzuna Takebe came together to form Sudannayuzuyully, a new take on female hip-hop. While performing as members of E-girls and Happiness, these three girls connected through their shared love of dance and hip-hop. They write and perform all of their own raps while staying true to the messages they want to convey. Their songwriting style comes down to rewriting lyrics and phrases until they sound perfect. Sudannayuzuyully is also part of the E.G. family.

Above:
Dream Ami

Opposite page:
Dream Aya

E-girls
Top row, left to right: Harumi Sato, Karen Fujii, Reina Washio, Yuzuna Takebe, and Kaede; Bottom row, left to right: Nonoka Yamaguchi, SAYAKA, Anna Suda, Nozomi Bando, YURINO, and Anna Ishii

This spread:
Happiness
Left to right:
MIYUU, YURINO, Karen Fujii, Anna Suda, Ruri Kawamoto, SAYAKA, and Kaede

Following spread:
Flower
Left to right:
Nozomi Bando, Shuuka Fujii, Mio Nakajima, Reina Washio, Manami Shigetome, and Harumi Sato

Previous spread:
ShuuKaRen
Left to right:
Karen Fujii, and
Shuuka Fujii

This spread:
Sudannayuzuyully
Left to right:
Anna Suda, Yuzuna
Takebe, and YURINO

Live Tour

"For years, we've focused all of our efforts on creating live performances that can entertain people from all backgrounds. Looking back, all that hard work has helped us get to where we are now. Our goals escalated year by year, starting from simply creating an entertaining show to creating something that could surprise the audience. Every year we would want to top ourselves, and now our shows have grown in scale so much so that I often hear reactions like 'this is crazy!' from non-Japanese audiences. It seems that we've become successful at surprising people all around the world."
— HIRO (from *THE ROAD TO EXILE TRIBE ~TOWER OF WISH~*, 2016)

In 2014, LDH created [EXILE TRIBE PERFECT YEAR], a project that featured more than thirteen LDH groups and artists, cumulatively drawing an audience of two million to their live shows that year. In 2015, the total number of fans who attended LDH performances since the company's founding reached over ten million. The annual "dome tour" alone can often consist of up to 41 different shows, some held at baseball stadiums with seating for up to 50,000 fans.

When HIRO started LDH as a company in 2002, his focus had always been on the music and how it would be performed live.

"To put it simply, I wanted our music and live shows to be better than anyone else's. Looking back, we didn't have much room to move financially, so we could only think about the short-term possibilities. For live performances, the core goal was to create something that can entertain the people who came out to the show. How can we make them feel satisfied with spending their own time and money to see us perform? EXILE's future depended on finding that answer, balancing what our fans wanted to see and what we wanted to do as artists. That was the starting point, and we've learned a lot since then."

It's a well-worn cliché but "putting everything on the line" remains the guiding principle for the EXILE approach to live performance to this day, and this is due in no large part because the company was established by HIRO and the other members, who were all performers by vocation. Their earliest shows, where making a profit wasn't the main goal, were always about the fans.

In the February 2016 issue of *GOETHE*, a Japanese men's interest magazine, HIRO added that "in order to create entertainment that can truly move an audience, it needs to be impactful in ways that not much else is. That's why we stretched ourselves to our limits, every single time. Creating a live performance that uses every drop of our potential has become the LDH way of doing things. Of course, every experience is something new, so mistakes and problems will arise, but each failure gives us a chance to take what we've learned and use that to improve our next show."

In recent years, LDH has begun renting out a stadium venue located in the Tohoku area of Japan to rehearse for their dome tours, complete with a set nearly identical to the final

Opposite page: HIRO backstage at a live show, 2015. Photography by Kei Ogata

Following spread: Rehearsals at Nagai Athletic Stadium, Osaka and Seibu Dome, Saitama. [EXILE LIVE TOUR 2010 FANTASY]

Coca-Cola Coca-Cola
大阪信用金庫

performance venue. To achieve this, they hire hundreds of rehearsal staff and bring in as many trucks filled with set pieces and equipment. Obviously, the cost is enormous, but that shows just how determined HIRO is when it comes to creating a successful live show.

Perhaps the most spectacular icon of these dome tours is the massive "Tower of Wish" first introduced in 2011. Utilized most recently in 2014 during [EXILE TRIBE PERFECT YEAR 2014], the structure is dominated by a four-legged tower rising to a height of 45 meters (148 feet), set on a 21-meter (70-foot) base that can deploy drawbridges and movable stages. Encircled halfway up its height by massive LED screens, "Tower of Wish" is the brainchild of the stage designer Kuniyoshi Ichikawa and his team at the agency Next One Create. A veteran of hundreds of arena tours for J-Pop powerhouses like AKB48, B'z, VAMPS, Tomoyasu Hotei and BOØWY, Ichikawa has worked with EXILE since 2007.

In an interview for the August/September 2012 cover story for the US-based trade publication *Live Design*, Ichikawa said he deployed the LED screens as a means of conveying visually to both fans and the performers this notion of "wish:" The wishes of the audience became the monument as the tower delivered a variety of expressions and messages with each song. Sometimes it showed something cool, sometimes it was comical and sometimes it was touching." He added, "I like a stage that surprises the audience by moving something that's not supposed to, so they don't get bored during 3-hour concerts. I was thinking that the outer stages and bridges would rotate together but also change speeds depending on the performance[1]."

"The scale of LDH's stage production has grown together with EXILE. In 2008, the stage production of EXILE's tour [EXILE PERFECT LIVE 2008] was the runner-up to Live Design *magazine's 2010 Excellence Award, which led to international recognition. Working with creatives around the world has taught me to be proud of our delicacy, precision, and hospitality. As LDH expands globally, our mission is to integrate the extravagance of global stage productions into the precision of shows that fully expresses 'Made In Japan' entertainment to the world.*

Taking inspiration and direction from HIRO, LDH Stage works to coordinate all elements of the live performance and works quickly with artists and staff to ensure that everything is succinct and top-notch. In addition, LDH stage conducts detailed research of performance venues, and develops a strong performance schedule to give our audiences a spectacular show. Aside from the planning and operations of LIVE performances of LDH artists, LDH Stage carries out all operational tasks, the organization of stage sets, design, lighting, and even coordination of rehearsals."
—LDH Stage CEO, Masanori Iemura

Opposite page:
[EXILE LIVE TOUR 2011 TOWER OF WISH], Kyocera Dome, Osaka

Follwing spread:
[EXILE TRIBE LIVE TOUR 2012 ~TOWER OF WISH~], Kyocera Dome, Osaka

P.80 81:
[EXILE LIVE TOUR 2015 "AMAZING WORLD"]

p.82-83:
[EXILE LIVE TOUR 2010 FANTASY], Hiroshima Big Arch, 2010

p.84:
TAKAHIRO in [EXILE LIVE TOUR 2015 "AMAZING WORLD"]

p.85:
AKIRA in [EXILE TRIBE LIVE TOUR 2012 ~TOWER OF WISH~]

p.86-87:
HIRO in [EXILE LIVE TOUR 2011 TOWER OF WISH]

[1] As told to David Johnson, "Exile on Main Street," *Live Design*, August/September 2012, p.30-34.

EXILE TRIBE

STAYGOLD

p.88:
MATSU (Toshio Matsumoto) in [EXILE LIVE TOUR 2011 TOWER OF WISH]

p.89:
HIRO in [EXILE LIVE TOUR 2011 TOWER OF WISH]

p.90:
[J Soul Brothers III from EXILE TRIBE LIVE TOUR 2015 "BLUE PLANET"]

p.91:
[EXILE LIVE TOUR 2015 "AMAZING WORLD"]

This spread:
AKIRA in [HiGH&LOW THE LIVE], 2016

p.94:
VERBAL in [HiGH&LOW THE LIVE], 2016

p.95:
SAMURIZE in [HiGH&LOW THE LIVE], 2016

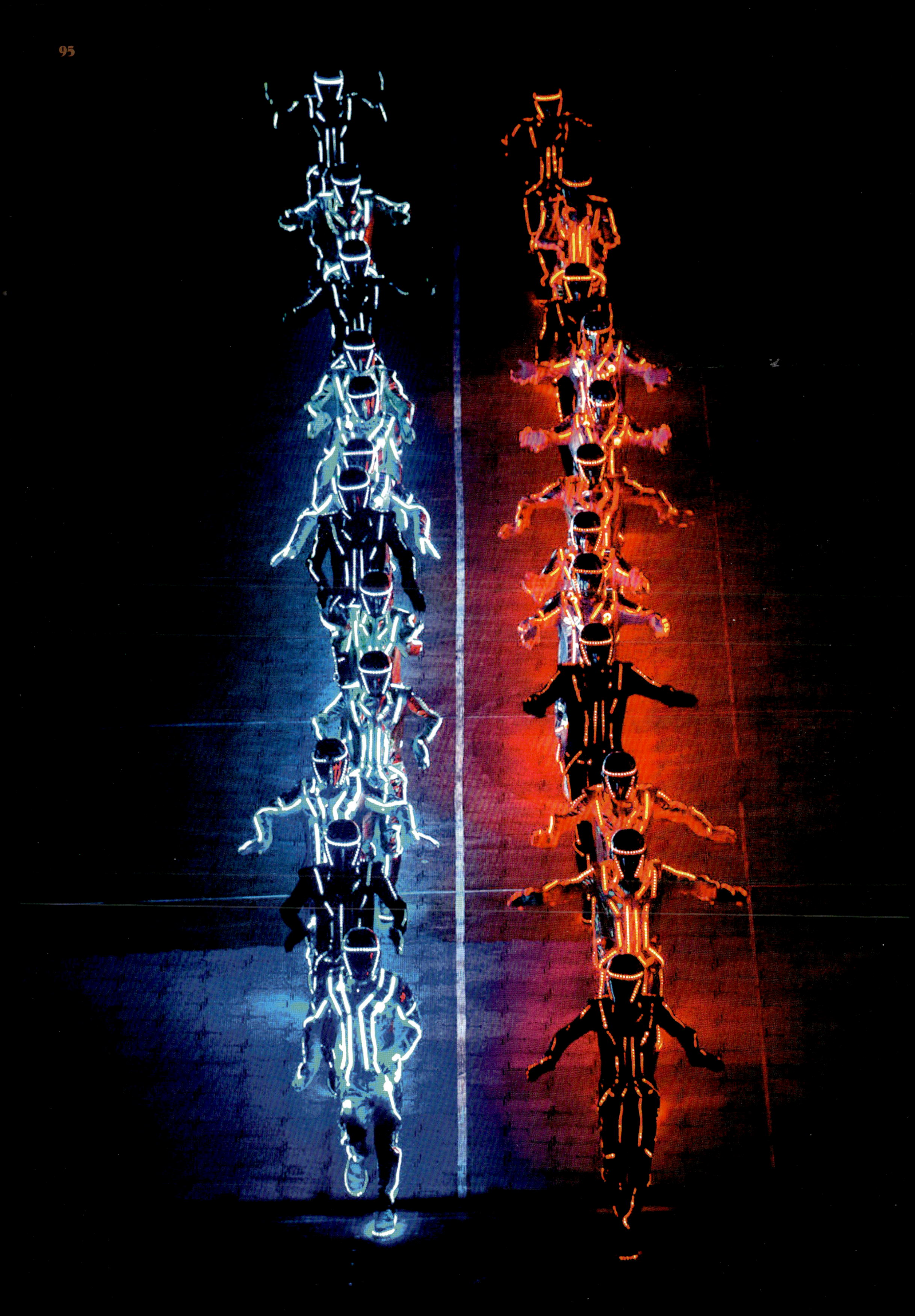

This spread:
[J Soul Brothers III from EXILE TRIBE LIVE TOUR 2015 "BLUE PLANET"]

p.98:
Top: ATSUSHI in [EXILE LIVE TOUR 2011 TOWER OF WISH];
Bottom: Hiroomi Tosaka and Ryuji Imaichi in [J Soul Brothers III from EXILE TRIBE LIVE TOUR 2015 "BLUE PLANET"]

p.99:
Top: TAKAHIRO in [EXILE LIVE TOUR 2011 TOWER OF WISH];
Bottom: MAKIDAI in [EXILE TRIBE LIVE TOUR 2012 ~TOWER OF WISH~]

p.100–101:
Backstage view of [J Soul Brothers III from EXILE TRIBE LIVE TOUR 2015 "BLUE PLANET"]

BUGATTI

ELLY
ELLY
STP

BOSCH
Spark Plugs
KAWASAKI
Scott
RACE
CREW
5

歩いてゆく道は
時につらくあって
生きるよろ
ソレが君の憧れになり
そして自分の全て
煌

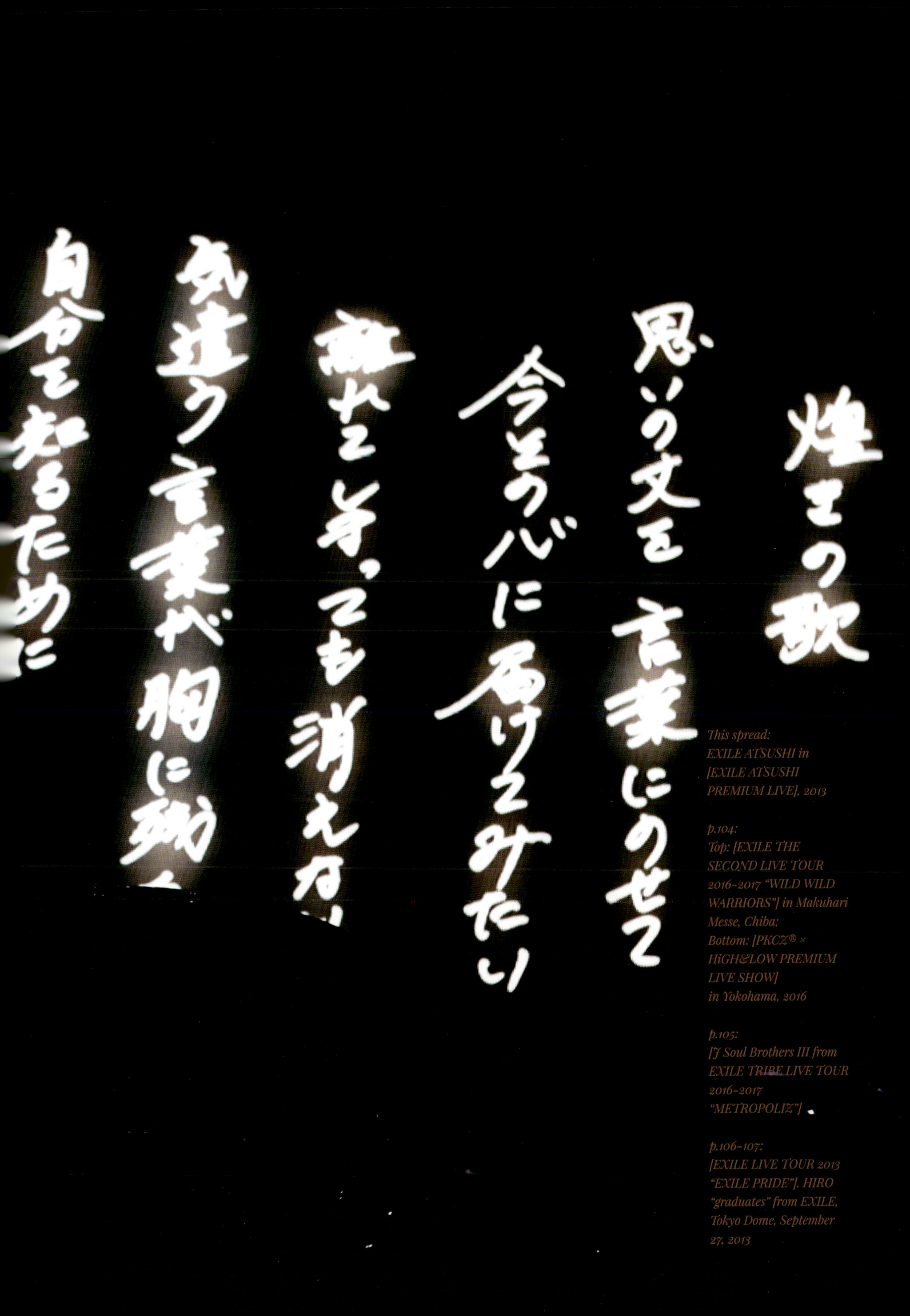

This spread:
EXILE ATSUSHI in [EXILE ATSUSHI PREMIUM LIVE], 2013

p.104:
Top: [EXILE THE SECOND LIVE TOUR 2016–2017 "WILD WILD WARRIORS"] in Makuhari Messe, Chiba;
Bottom: [PKCZ® × HiGH&LOW PREMIUM LIVE SHOW] in Yokohama, 2016

p.105:
[J Soul Brothers III from EXILE TRIBE LIVE TOUR 2016–2017 "METROPOLIZ"]

p.106–107:
[EXILE LIVE TOUR 2013 "EXILE PRIDE"]. HIRO "graduates" from EXILE, Tokyo Dome, September 27, 2013

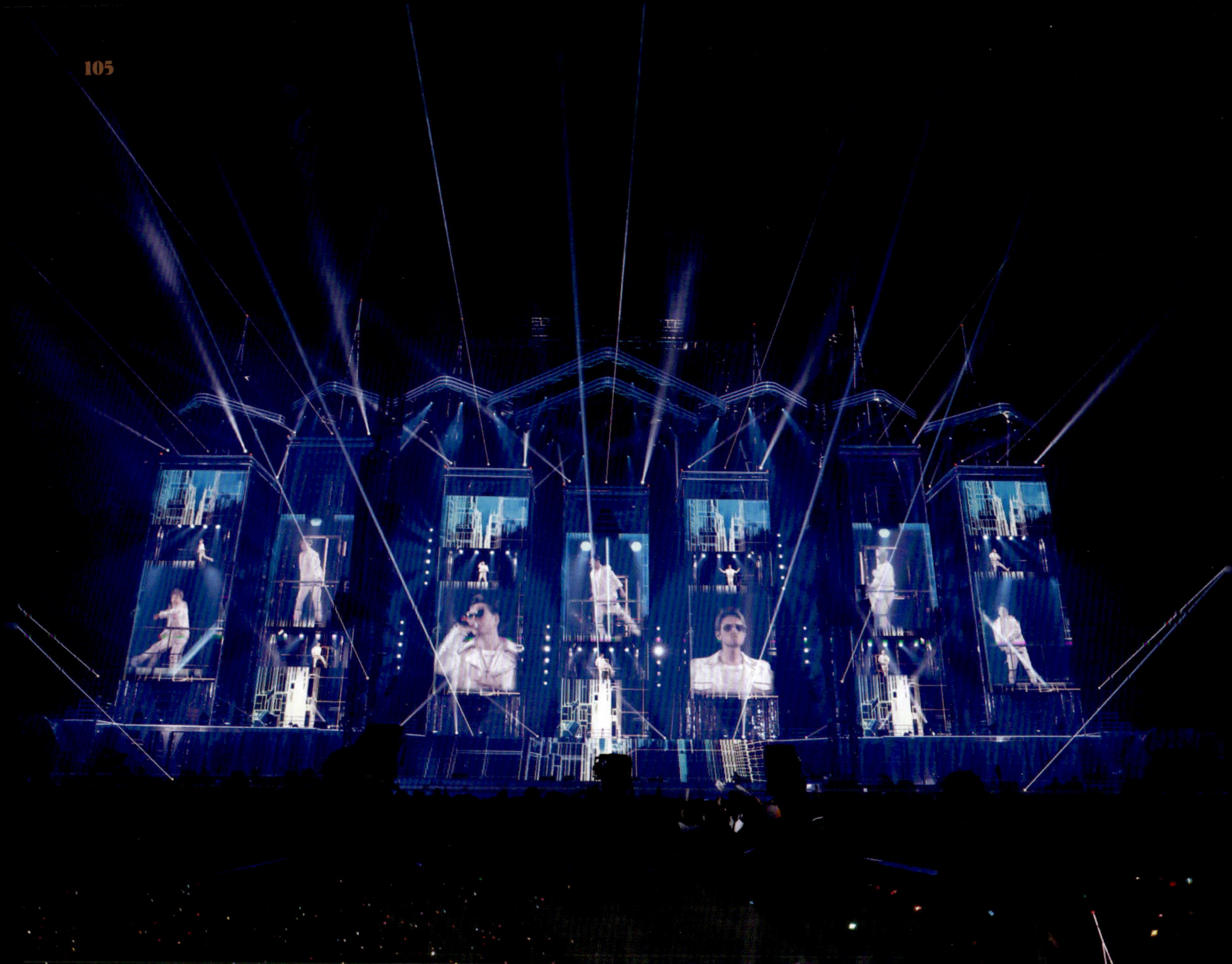

116253
22G1

Fashion & Apparel

"LDH Apparel and LDH Kitchen were both founded because our childhood friends had been pursuing their careers as designers and chefs. Today, this has led our artists to fulfill their own dreams of producing fashion brands and coffee shops. Every project within both LDH Apparel and LDH Kitchen are intertwined with our artists' and staffs' involvement, and we do not think of them as independent businesses."
— HIRO

With overseas collaborations, LDH will approach the world market.

"Originally established to develop rehearsal gear for EXILE, the commercial success of "24karats" laid the foundation for the establishment of LDH Apparel. With direct input from LDH artists and a strong mission to create products of the highest quality, LDH Apparel has continued to impact the industry with innovative changes in fashion. As we leap into the global market, we will be collaborating with international creatives to introduce what we have to offer to the global market. By building infrastructure in local regions we can also change the fashion landscape by tailoring our designs to each country and customer."
—LDH Apparel CEO, Satoshi Ogawa

Performance and fashion share the same creative spirit.

"Communicating with the LDH Apparel staff and keeping an open mind has allowed me to express my love for fashion. In 2015, HIRO gave me the opportunity to produce my own brand "Studio Seven" and truly become a part of LDH Apparel. Although I have always been an active member of the decision-making process, this new role at LDH Apparel allows me to have a direct impact and communicate the heart and philosophy of EXILE with the entire team."
—LDH Apparel, EXILE NAOTO

LDH Apparel is responsible for the fashion brands "24karats" "J.S.B." "EG" "STUDIO SEVEN" "FULLBK" and "Enasoluna" with "PKCZ® GALLERY STORE" being the official retail space. Born from LDH rehearsal wear, LDH-produced apparel eventually progressed to exposure in music videos and live shows. A strong demand among fans led to the creation of "24karats" and many other brands. LDH Apparel is an essential platform which allows artists to share their creative vision with fans through apparel and style.

Opposite page and following page: HIRO, photographed by Kei Ogata, in 24karats × MASTERMIND collaboration, 2013

Opposite page:
24karats 2016 A/W COLLECTION: Photography: Yuichi Akagi, Styling: Masataka Hattori

Following spread:
24karats 2017 S/S COLLECTION: Photography: Keita Suzuki; Styling: Lambda Takahashi

p.114–115:
24karats 2014 A/W COLLECTION: Photography: Mitsuo Okamoto; Styling: Lambda Takahashi; Hair & make-up: Masanori Kobayashi

p.116–117:
24karats 2016 A/W COLLECTION: Photography: Kiyotaka Hatanaka; Styling: Lambda Takahashi; Hair & make-up: Shinya Kawamura

BALLIN!!
TWO FOUR

JSB
74 83 66

JSB
74 83 66

Previous spread:
J.S.B. 2016 COLLECTION; Photography: Keita Suzuki; Styling: Atsushi Hashimoto

This spread:
J.S.B. 2017 S/S COLLECTION; Photography: Shunya Arai; Styling: Yasuhiro Watanabe

p.122–123:
Image of PKCZ® Gallery Store in Nakameguro, Tokyo

p.124–125:
STUDIO SEVEN SEASON 3 (2017 A/W); Photography: Liam Wong; Styling: Lambda Takahashi; Hair & make-up: Masanori Kobayashi

p.126–127:
STUDIO SEVEN SEASON 1 (2015 A/W); Photography: Shunya Arai; Styling: Lambda Takahashi; Hair & make-up: Go Takakusagi

p.128–129:
STUDIO SEVEN SEASON 1 (2015 A/W); Photography: Shunya Arai; Styling: Lambda Takahashi; Hair & make-up: Go Takakusagi

J.S.B.
J.S.B.

PKCZ.
GALLERY STORE

PKCZ®
GALLERY STORE

北海道
牛
牛
小澤牧場
GYUMARU
042-521-2785

Humanmade for
SEVEN

separation

SEPARATION KILLS US
MMXVII
AMIGOS

ZING WORLD
ILE TOUR

*p.130:
HUMAN MADE × STUDIO SEVEN (2016 S/S); art direction by NIGO®*

*p.131:
HUMAN MADE × STUDIO SEVEN (2017 A/W), featuring NAOTO; art direction by NIGO®*

*p.132–133:
FULL-BK (2017 A/W); Photography: Katsuhide Morimoto; Styling: Lambda Takahashi; Hair & make-up: Taro Yoshida*

*p.134–135:
FULL-BK (2016 S/S); Photography: Kazuki Nagayama; Styling: Lambda Takahashi; Hair & make-up: Masanori Kobayashi*

*p.136–137:
Stage outfit exclusively designed by AMBUSH® for [J Soul Brothers III from EXILE TRIBE LIVE TOUR 2016–2017 "METROPOLIZ"], 2016, featuring NAOTO (p.136) and Ryuji Imaichi (p.137)*

*p.138–139:
Rings, bangle, necklace and collar designed by Enasoluna, A/W 2015 Collection; Photography by Yuji Takeuchi (p.138) and Asa Sato (p.139)*

*This page and following spread:
Hoodie and Nylon Jacket, tour goods from [EXILE LIVE TOUR 2015" AMAZING WORLD"]. Photography by Keita Suzuki*

EXILE PRIDE
LIVE TOUR 2013
EXILE
LIVE TOUR 2010
FANTASY
EXILE
PERFECT
YEAR
EXILE
VOCAL BATTLE
AUDITION
2006 ~ASIAN DREAM~
Styles of Beyond
LOVE DR

EXILE TRIBE
LIVE TOUR 2012
TOWER OF WISH
EXILE
THE
MONSTER
LIVE TOUR 2009
EXILE
SHOWCASE LIVE
2 0 0 8
EXILE
LIVE TOUR 2005
PERFECT LIVE ASIA
APPINESS

This spread:
Exterior and interior of EXILE TRIBE STATION store, 2016, located in Nakameguro, Tokyo

Merchandise—often fully designed and produced by LDH artists themselves—is sold at EXILE's live shows. Apparel, novelties and books are designed and curated with unique wit and humor. It was by design that the development of these tour goods have direct input from the artists, and have, in their own way, become a form of LDH entertainment. Goods are sold through EXILE TRIBE STATION, as well as mobile platforms

Film & Theater

"EXILE's unique spirit has been condensed through the perspective of a traditional movie. Although the movie itself is a historical film, *Tatara Samurai* conveys the notion that the most important things in life do not change over time. In fact, we believe that the message will resonate even more because of the age that we live in today. We would like to continue to show this side of EXILE, and we are proud to present this film to everyone."
—HIRO

Shot on location in Shimane Prefecture in southern Honshu and directed by Yoshinori Nishikori, the period film was released in Japan on May 20, 2017 and was recently awarded Best International Feature at the 2017 UK Screen One International Film Festival and Best Artistic Contribution at the 2017 Montreal World Film Festival.

Set during the late Sengoku period, an era of political upheaval and constant warfare, it is the story of Gosuke, a young man torn between remaining a *murage*, a master blacksmith and guardian of an ancient steel and sword-making tradition in the small village of Tatara, and becoming a samurai to fend off raids by the various warring clans that covet the indestructible and stainless steel made there.

In describing the impossible choices imposed by war on a man of peace, Andy Weber in his June 1, 2017 review for the *New York Times* praised the film's direction: "Yoshinori Nishikori's period action film does not skimp with its swordplay, but its narrative arc takes you to a resolution uncommon for its genre… Best of all, his hero, played with a quiet, nuanced gravity by Mr. Aoyagi, does not become a superhuman warrior but rather a weary veteran aspiring to civilization's higher ideals."

In his previous film *Konshin* (2013), Nishikori made a gutsy move in casting a lesser-known actor, Sho Aoyagi as his lead after a single audition. This caught the attention of the actor's management company, LDH, and HIRO, as Aoyagi is a crucial member of Gekidan EXILE, the theatrical troupe of EXILE TRIBE (see pages 158–159). Following their first meeting, EXILE HIRO and Nishikori immediately hit it off, and began exchanging ideas on a variety of film ideas. Among the treatments discussed, HIRO expressed the most interest in developing *Tatara Samurai*.

During the production of this film, HIRO made numerous trips to Shimane Prefecture, and to the artisanal furnaces that inherited the *tatara-buki* and the *tamagahane* techniques so lovingly described in the film. These visits roused in him a sense of splendor towards the natural beauty of the surrounding region, which is at once coastal and mountainous, and Shimane's unique cultural heritage.

The director and LDH Pictures assembled a veteran crew, including artistic director Noriyoshi Ikeya, director of photography Akira Sakou and lighting designer Sousuke Yoshikado. A

p.146–155: Stills from "Tatara Samurai" (2016), featuring Sho Aoyagi, AKIRA, Naoki Kobayashi, Masahiko Tsugawa, Tomoko Naraoka, Kei Yamamoto, Choei Takahashi, Takashi Sasano, Toru Shinagawa, Yoshiko Miyazaki, Masahiro Komoto, Kosuke Toyohara, and Denden. The film was shot on location in Shimane Prefecture, and directed by Yoshinori Nishikori

team of traditional carpenters, woodworkers and architectural advisors built an open set near the town of Okuizumo, recreating a feudal hamlet with an authentic forge at its heart. Throughout the filming a master blacksmith advised actors on set.

Accompanying Sho Aoyagi, an esteemed group of seasoned actors—including Masahiko Tsugawa, Tomoko Naraoka, Kei Yamamoto, Choei Takahashi, Takashi Sasano, Toru Shinagawa, Yoshiko Miyazaki, Masahiro Komoto, Kosuke Toyohara, and Denden—are supplemented by the crucial participation of EXILE TRIBE members AKIRA and Naoki Kobayashi, who were both cast in major roles.

Of particular note, the director and cinematographer chose to film in Panavision, a format that is used less and less on Japanese films, and imported a camera that was used recently on Hollywood blockbusters. Nishikori remarked on the use of analog film after filming the last scene: "We haven't done anything ground-breaking. We have only been following in the footsteps of our movie-making predecessors while choosing to pay particular attention to details."

CINEMA FIGHTERS (see pages 156–157) is a project that invited a number of spirited filmmakers to create short films of up to twenty minutes in length using tracks from artists who are part of EXILE TRIBE. After partnering with actors, EXILE TRIBE members and Tetsuya Bessho's short films brand Short Shorts, a total of six short films by six different directors, including Naomi Kawase, were created using LDH tracks written by lyricist Masato Odake. The films premiered at Short Shorts Film Festival & Asia (SSFF&ASIA), an Academy Awards-accredited festival, in June 2017.

Under the Black Dress
Director: Toshimichi Saito; Runtime: 12 mins.; Song: "Dress wo Nuida Cinderella" by Dream Ami; Cast: Dream Ami, and Takeshi Kaga

Destination
Director: Shiro Tokiwa; Runtime: 20 mins.; Song: "HANABI" by J Soul Brother's III from EXILE TRIBE; Cast: Keita Machida, Hyunri, Yanagi Elisa, and Kanji Furutachi

Swan Song
Director: Ken Ochiai; Runtime: 17 mins.; Song: "Heavenly White" by EXILE; Cast: Takanori Iwata, and Nanami Sakuraba

CINEMA FIGHTERS

EXILE TRIBE × SHORTSHORTS

エグゼクティブプロデューサー: EXILE HIRO

企画・プロデュース: 別所哲也

コンセプトプロデューサー: 小竹正人

配給:LDH PICTURES

「パラレルワールド」
作品原案曲:「Unfair World」by 三代目 J Soul Brothers from EXILE TRIBE
監督・脚本:河瀬直美　キャスト:山田孝之 / 石井杏奈

「キモチラボの解法」
作品原案曲:「白雪姫」by Flower
監督・脚本:A.T.　キャスト:AKIRA / 小林喜日 / 駒井蓮 / 水崎綾女

「Snowman」
作品原案曲:「Mr.Snowman」by E-girls
監督・脚本:萩原健太郎　キャスト:倍賞美津子 / 鈴木伸之 / 藤井美菜 / 村井國夫

「色のない洋服店」
作品原案曲:「ドレスを脱いだシンデレラ」by Dream Ami
監督・脚本:齋藤俊道　キャスト:Dream Ami / 鹿賀丈史

「終着の場所」
作品原案曲:「花火」by 三代目 J Soul Brothers from EXILE TRIBE
監督・脚本:常盤司郎　キャスト:町田啓太 / 玄理

「SWAN SONG」
作品原案曲:「Heavenly White」by EXILE
監督・脚本:落合賢　キャスト:岩田剛典 / 桜庭ななみ

6.1 [Thu] ショートショート フィルムフェスティバル & アジア 2017 にてプレミア上映

LDH JAPAN　LDH Pictures　Pacific Voice　SHORTSHORTS FILM FESTIVAL & ASIA

EXILE TRIBE
PATERSON CITY 66

GEKIDAN EXILE

(EXILE THEATER COMPANY)

Consistent with EXILE's founding principles, aspiring actors, particularly those interested in pursuing a career in theater are provided the support they need to make their dreams reality within LDH. To help achieve this goal, the company formed the performance troupe GEKIDAN EXILE Hanagumi in August 2008, followed by Kazegumi in 2010. These groups focused on stage acting, in both plays, musicals, all the while incorporating aspects of EXILE's three main themes of "love, dream, and happiness" in their varied performances.

The Hanagumi and Kazegumi troupes eventually came together to form what is now known as GEKIDAN EXILE, a group home to popular actors who are featured in a wide variety of mainstream movies and TV dramas as well as traditional theater.

Members include Sho Aoyagi, Shintaro Akiyama, Yuta Ozawa, Nobuyuki Suzuki, Keita Machida, Hayato Onozuka, Shuhei Nogae, Masayasu Yagi, and Kanta Sato.

Above:
Top row, left to right: Nobuyuki Suzuki, Sho Aoyagi, Keita Machida, and Kanta Sato;
Bottom row, left to right: Shintaro Akiyama, Yuta Ozawa, Hayato Onozuka, Masayasu Yagi, and Shuhei Nogae

Opposite page:
Top: GEKIDAN EXILE performance of Sore Ike Shogekijo!! *(October 2014);*
Middle: GEKIDAN EXILE performance of Mayuge Ichizoku no Inbo, *a spoken-word drama developed from* Attack No.1 *(April 2014);*
Bottom: Attack No.1, *performed in collaboration with Hounangumi theater company (July 2015)*

HIGH

& LOW

CREATED & PRODUCED BY HIRO & STARRING THE ENTIRE EXILE TRIBE, HIGH&LOW IS LDH'S PURSUIT OF THE NEXT LEVEL OF ENTERTAINMENT THROUGH A VARIETY OF MEDIA INCLUDING TV DRAMAS, FEATURE FILMS, LIVE TOURS, SOUNDTRACKS, MUSIC VIDEOS, POP-UP RESTAURANTS, COMICS AND SOCIAL MEDIA CONTENT.

若一家

NBHD
ORIGINAL

HIGH&LOW: CONCEPT

"HiGH&LOW is a project that was borne out of the EXILE TRIBE members' dreams of surprising the world and providing excitement for our fans. As we shared our experiences as performers, ideas began to blossom, eventually leading to the launch of this exciting project.

'Love, Dream, Happiness' is the motto that serves as the foundation to our work, but this project is completely different, at least on the surface, from how we've expressed it so far in our live shows and other productions. With this project, we will deliver 'Love, Dream, Happiness' from a totally different angle.

With HiGH&LOW we hope to unveil forms of entertainment that the fans can truly say they have not experienced or seen before."—HIRO

Initially introduced in the Fall of 2015 with TV drama series on the terrestrial Nippon Television channel (NTV), the sprawling gangland epic HiGH&LOW has become a mini media empire within LDH. Incorporating a variety of genres—from TV Dramas, feature films, live tours, soundtracks, music videos, pop-up restaurants, comics and social media content—the project utilizes not only the entirety of the EXILE TRIBE but also all the resources of LDH, under the overall direction of HIRO and the filmmaker Shigeaki Kubo.

HiGH&LOW [THE STORY OF S.W.O.R.D.] began as a 10-episode TV series in October 2015. It was renewed for a second 10-episode season in April 2016, both broadcast on NTV with a simultaneous "director's cut" available on Hulu Japan.

Leading up to the movie premiere in Japan on July 16, 2016, an original soundtrack featuring various artists from the groups of EXILE TRIBE was released, subsequently followed by a live stadium tour that began at Osaka's Kyocera Dome on July 22.

THE ROAD TO HIGH&LOW: T.V. DRAMA

The "HiGH&LOW" project began with a TV drama. Broadcast on terrestrial TV, seasons 1 and 2 were also syndicated on Hulu Japan. In advance of the July 2016 release of *HiGH&LOW The Movie*, a theatrical feature condensing events from the TV series, *THE ROAD TO HiGH&LOW* was released on May 7, 2016.

THE ROAD TO HiGH&LOW describes the origins of powerful gangs that would ultimately fight for control of a vast territory in a coastal town. The core of the story is the relationship between Cobra (Takanori Iwata), Yamato (Nobuyuki Suzuki) and Noboru (Keita Machida). Friends since childhood, Noboru is a good student who attends college, and provides some direction to both Cobra and Yamato, who seem to be good only at fighting. When tragedy leads to Noboru's departure, Cobra and Yamato form the Sanno Rengokai (Sanno Federation) in anticipation of his return.

A second, parallel arc tells of the rise of the Mugen family, which also began with lifelong friends Kohaku (EXILE AKIRA) and Tatsuya (Arata Iura). United by a passion for motorcycles, this association would in time include Ota (Hiroyuki Takaya), Konishi (Yushin Okami) and Tsukumo (Sho Aoyagi). With the ascendance of Mugen as a dominant faction, its rivalry with another biker gang headed by the Amamiya Brothers (played by EXILE TAKAHIRO and Hiroomi Tosaka) would set up the central conflict in *HiGH&LOW The Movie*.

HIGH&LOW: THE MOVIE

p.160-161: Still from *HiGH&LOW The Movie* (2016), featuring Takanori Iwata (as Cobra) and EXILE AKIRA (as Kohaku)
p.162-163: Still from *HiGH&LOW THE STORY OF S.W.O.R.D.*, TV series for NTV (2015) featuring Kento Hayashi
p.164: Poster for the theatrical release of *HiGH&LOW The Movie* (2016)
p.165: [HiGH&LOW THE LIVE] in Tokyo Dome, 2016
p.166: Stills from *ROAD TO HiGH&LOW*, a 2016 theatrical release that condenses Season 1 (*HiGH&LOW THE STORY OF S.W.O.R.D.*) and Season 2 of the TV series. Images feature Kenchi Tachibana and Keita Machida (p.166, left to right), Keita Machida, Nobuyuki Suzuki and Takanori Iwata (p.167 top, left to right), Sho Aoyagi and EXILE AKIRA (p.167 bottom, left to right)
This spread: Still from *HiGH&LOW The Movie* (2016) featuring the gangs of S.W.O.R.D.

Released in Japan by Shochiku on July 16, 2016 and directed by Shigeaki Kubo, *HiGH&LOW The Movie* debuted at number 2 in its opening weekend after Disney's *Finding Dory*.

An unnamed town once ruled by the Mugen gang has been split into five rival districts after a group lead by the Amamiya Brothers (played by EXILE TAKAHIRO and Hiroomi Tosaka) refused to submit to their control. With the dissolution of Mugen, the five groups that emerged from the chaos took their names from each of the letters that comprise the renamed territory S.W.O.R.D.: Sanno Rengokai (Sanno Federation), White Rascals, Oya Koh (Oya High School), Rude Boys, and the Daruma Ikka.

The ensuing power struggle is complicated by the arrival of a mysterious group, the Mighty Warriors, and the return of the legendary Mugen warrior Kohaku (EXILE AKIRA) and his allies in the Infinity faction, Tsukumo (Sho Aoyagi) and Lee (V.I of the K-pop juggernaut Big Bang). At the head of five hundred warriors, they are opposed by a coalition headed by the Amamiya Brothers, the Sanno Federation and the other gangs of the S.W.O.R.D. district.

Additional cast members include Takanori Iwata, Nobuyuki Suzuki, Kenjiro Yamashita, Keita Machida, Taiki Sato, Kanta Sato, Keiji Kuroki, Kiryuin Sho, Kyan Yutaka, Utahiroba Jun, Darvish Kenji, Reo Sano Karen Fujii, ELLY, Shuhei Nogae, Taichi Saotome, Alan Shirahama, ANARCHY, and Kana Oya, Kenchi Tachibana, Shintaro Akiyama, Yuta Ozawa, Masayasu Yagi, Hayato Onozuka.

MightyWarriors

DINER

HiGH&LOW THE BASE

HiGH&LOW:

THE RED RAIN

The story of the Amamiya brothers, who lost their parents at a young age: Masaki Amamiya (EXILE TAKAHIRO), the youngest brother who hid his emotions from the others; Hiroto Amamiya (Hiroomi Tosaka), the middle brother; and Takeru Amamiya, the wise eldest brother who kept them all together. They were bestowed a teaching before their parents' passing: "The fist can only be used to protect your loved ones." All three vowed to protect one another. But Takeru mysteriously disappears and his younger brothers begin a search for him. Hoping to find him at their parents' graves, they instead meet a young girl, Aika Naruse (Miyu Yoshimoto), at the cemetery, who carries a clue to Takeru's whereabouts and joins in their quest. Through their journey, the truth behind the dark past of the Amamiya brothers is revealed.

END OF SKY

Peace in the S.W.O.R.D. district has once again come to an end. Ranmaru Hayashi (Aoi Nakamura), leader of the DOUBT gang, feared for his violence and cruelty, is released from prison. Ranmaru set out to crush the White Rascals—a group led by Rocky, who split with Ranmaru because he could no longer tolerate his brutality. Cobra and the Sanno Federation also join in the fray. Other leaders of S.W.O.R.D. agree to join forces to protect their families.

Meanwhile, Kohaku and the Amamiya Brothers obtain evidence that a shadowy group, the Kuryu, have conspired to build a casino in the S.W.O.R.D. district, with plans to wrest control of the whole territory. But before Kohaku and the Amamiyas can bring this scheme to light, a lieutenant of the Kuryu Group, Genji (Naoki Kobayashi) attacks them.

Above: Still from *HiGH&LOW THE RED RAIN* (2016) featuring EXILE TAKAHIRO, Takumi Saito, and Hiroomi Tosaka.
Opposite page: Views of HiGH&LOW THE BASE, a pop-up "theme park" that ran for two months in 2016.
Following spread: Still from *HiGH&LOW THE MOVIE II / END OF SKY* (2017), featuring NAOTO.

Eat to live,
and not live to eat.

175

HIGH&LOW: THE MUSIC

To match the energy and the vibe of the film series a corresponding "Best Album" was created and packaged together as part of the media project. Artists on the album include many LDH artists (J Soul Brothers III, EXILE THE SECOND, GENERATIONS, E-girls, ACE OF SPADES, PKCZ® and DOBERMAN INFINITY, among others). As the film series is such a large-scale project, LDH wanted to join together as many artists to inspire and present this ambitious, multimedia entertainment.

In addition to LDH artists, overseas artists joined the roster to create the soundtrack. Dimitri Vegas & Like Mike produced *HiGH&LOW The Movie* and *HiGH&LOW The Movie II*'s main themes. Additional guests included Afrojack, V.I (from BIGBANG) and Far East Movement. This international, all-star lineup created a supercharged sound in keeping with the scale of the film series and the fictional world in which it is set, which was shot in Japan and the Philippines.

This spread: Stills from "HIGHER GROUND feat. Dimitri Vegas & Like Mike" by EXILE TRIBE, featuring TAKAHIRO and EXILE TRIBE, 2016.
Following spread: Still from *HiGH&LOW THE MOVIE* (2016), featuring (L-F) ANARCHY, Kana Oya, ELLY and SWAY.

Music Videos

"Our focus on creating a sense of realism comes directly from who we are. Whether in music videos or during live performances, we always focus on what's 'real.' Even fantasy can feel realistic if you make sure all the minute details feel true. My favorite movies and TV shows are those that are rooted in reality."
— HIRO (from *THE ROAD TO EXILE TRIBE ~TOWER OF WISH~*, 2016)

Shigeaki Kubo is the director behind more than 100 music videos for LDH artists. His mission is to realize HIRO's grand ideas for music videos on film. His mission is to realize HIRO's grand ideas for music videos on film.

"I learned this after the fact, but when HIRO was searching for a new music video director in 2008, he brought up three music videos as examples for what he was looking for, and it turns out that I directed all three of them. That led to him contacting me, and ever since, I have been directing music videos for not only EXILE but for EXILE TRIBE groups as well.

I have huge respect for music and those who create it, and my mentality when working on music videos is to portray the idea that music can change the world. However, it's difficult to experience the true magic and emotion of a song until it's performed right in front of you, so I think of music videos as tools to bring people together and encourage them to see their favorite artists live. The best way to enjoy music is at a live venue, connecting and sharing your experiences with like-minded people. But at the same time, another one of my goals is to create music videos that not only envelop the emotion and intensity of the live performances, but also overcome them. I believe music videos are about expanding the artists' worldview, while at the same time complementing the artists' live performances."

Opposite page:
Stills from "S.A.K.U.R.A." by J Soul Brothers III from EXILE TRIBE, 2014

This page: Stills from "Flower Song" by EXILE, 2013

Opposite page: Stills from "PERFORMER'S PRIDE" by EXILE, 2013

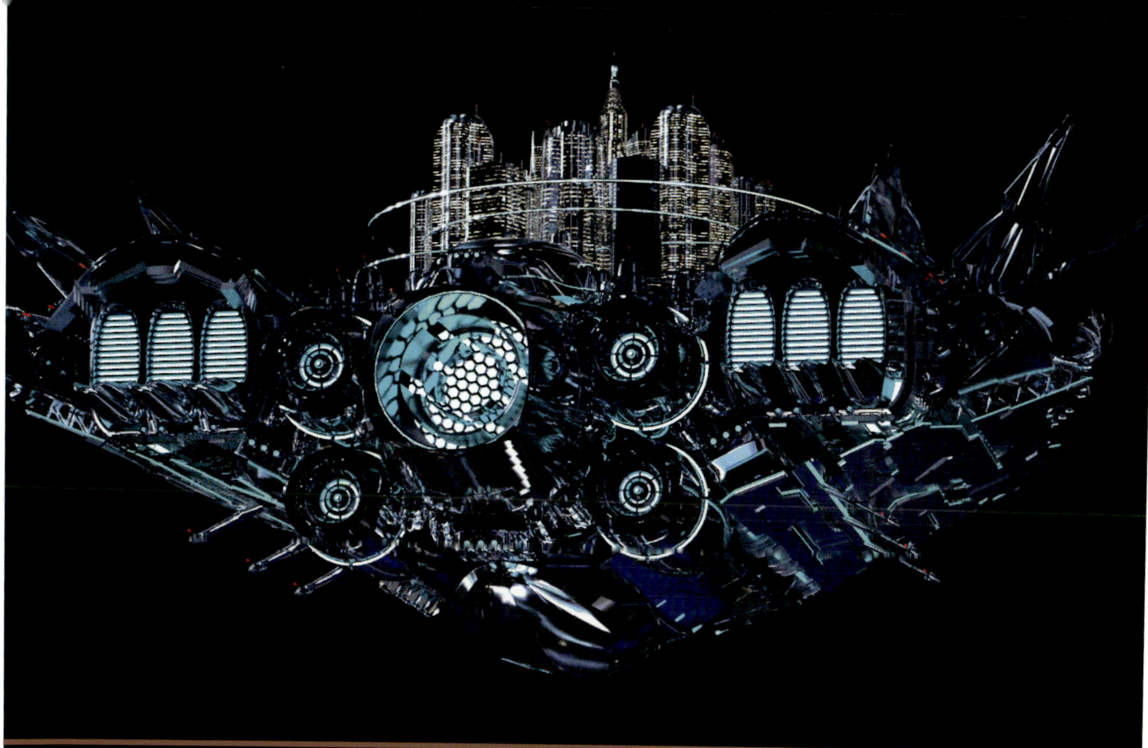

Opposite page:
Stills from
"24karats TRIBE OF GOLD"
by EXILE, 2012

This page:
Stills from
"EXILE PRIDE" Konna Sekai wo Aisuru Tameni (To Love a World Such as We Live In)" by EXILE, 2013

This page: Stills from "No Limit" by EXILE, 2013

Opposite page: Still from "RYDEEN ~Dance All Night~" by E-girls, 2014

Still from the animated projection of the character Genesis from [EXILE TRIBE PERFECT YEAR 2014 SPECIAL STAGE "THE SURVIVAL" IN SAITAMA SUPER ARENA 10 DAYS]

Dance Studios

NEW YORK

Previous spread:
EXPG NY, 2015

This page:
Top: Reception, EXPG STUDIO Tokyo, 2017;
Middle: Vocal studio, EXPG STUDIO Tokyo, 2017;
Bottom: Dance studio, EXPG STUDIO Tokyo, 2017

Opposite page:
EXPG NY exterior, opened in 2014

"To EXILE, EXPG STUDIO is itself a form of entertainment, and a place for new encounters. The energy that I felt when I first danced in front of an audience, back when I still had no clue what I was doing, is what keeps me going to this day.

I had always taught dance, and a variety of chance encounters and happy coincidences throughout my life gave me the opportunity to perform on the big stage. I feel honored to be able to encourage younger talent with the same aspirations through EXPG STUDIO. I believe that this positive energy will rebound to me and lead to even more encounters. This is our way of contributing to society, and I wish for those who feel the same way to join us."
— HIRO

EXPG STUDIO is a full-scale entertainment school dedicated to helping young artists grow through lessons that include dance, vocal performance, acting, and more.

EXPG STUDIO TOKYO was opened in 2003 as a place where children who dream of becoming international entertainers come to follow in EXILE's footsteps. Since, the school has expanded across cities in Japan including Miyazaki, Sapporo, Osaka, Matsuyama, Fukuoka, Okinawa, Nagoya, Yokohama, Omiya, Kyoto, and Sendai, as well as overseas locations in Taipei and New York. In total, EXPG STUDIO includes 14 schools, twelve in Japan and two overseas, with new schools expected to open in Los Angeles and Shanghai in 2018.

One of EXPG STUDIO's defining characteristics is that the curriculum is built around the goal of creating professional entertainers, taught by instructors with years of experience as professionals in their respective fields. Numerous graduates have gone on to find professional success, many of whom return to the school to conduct special lectures and show current students what is possible through hard work and dedication.

The goal for EXPG STUDIO's lessons and curriculum isn't just to help students improve their dance skills. The primary goal is for students to believe in themselves while sharing their passion for performing with their peers, connections that LDH hopes will lead to lifelong friendships and even vocational relationships.

Opposite page:
EXPG Tokyo, 2015

This page:
Middle and bottom: EXPG NY, featuring dancers Henry Link and Buddha Stretch

This page:
Top to bottom: [HOUSE OF EXILE] at Stage 48, NYC, 2015. Middle photo features the dancer Sam O.

Opposite page:
Omarion and crew at [HOUSE OF EXILE], 2015

HOUSE OF EXILE

Top performers and street dancers from around the world convene annually in New York to attend this unique event. With an emphasis on styles that evolved from hip-hop, such as breakdancing, turfing and krumping, the show includes dance performances, dance battles, and performances by special musical guests. The inaugural HOUSE OF EXILE was held in 2015, and along with a number of other LDH events and initiatives, has received considerable acclaim for invigorating the tradition of the dance battle as a must-see event in Manhattan and introducing it to a global audience.

Event attendees have included New York's legendary MOP TOP CREW, internationally popular choreographers Shaun Evaristo and Lyle Beniga, as well as up-and-coming stars like Ayo and Teo, Kida The Great, and Ysabelle Captile. The event celebrates how street dance has evolved over the years, and what the future holds for the genre.

The dance battles bring together world-renowned battlers from as far afield as Europe, Latin America and Asia for an intense night of competition, with the high level of technique on display blowing away audience expectations year on year. Winners of past events include Spider Salah and one of the pioneers of krump, Tight Eyez.

Renowned American artists take up the guest performance slots each year, with past performers including Raekwon of the Wu-Tang Clan, Swizz Beatz, Busta Rhymes, Omarion, Tinashe, Lil' Kim, and many others. LDH artists from Japan have also lit up the stage, including CRAZYBOY, Crystal Kay, DEEP, and Jr. Exile from PROJECT TARO. HOUSE OF EXILE has become an international platform to promote LDH's unique style of entertainment. Acknowledging the enormous influence of New York on his own development as a performer, HIRO fully intends it to become a local tradition as well.

Opposite page: Crystal Kay at [HOUSE OF EXILE], 2016.

This page: Top: Raekwon of the Wu-Tang Clan, at [HOUSE OF EXILE], 2016; Middle: Performers of PROJECT TARO. Bottom: Sekai and Loose Joint

Cuisine

"In the end, it's all about the person. LDH owes its success to the people I've been able to meet in my life. Creating something only has true meaning when it is done with somebody who shares the same spirit, and meeting them in person is the only way to find out. LDH has always treasured this spirit... LDH Kitchen, our restaurant branch, was also founded with a classmate who was pursuing his career as a chef, to create restaurants where our artists can casually dine."
— HIRO

"LDH Kitchen strives to create a unique blend of food and entertainment. LDH currently serves a variety of cuisines throughout our restaurants, and our goal is for each restaurant to celebrate its unique aspects, and accommodate elements of entertainment to provide an unforgettable experience. As of this writing, LDH Kitchen plans to open its first restaurant overseas, in Los Angeles, with an aim to blend the beauty of Japanese cuisine with that city's diverse food culture. Along with our annual summer tradition "Izakaya EXILE PARK," LDH Kitchen strives to create amazing culinary experiences to our fans."
—LDH Kitchen CEO, Hiroyuki Suzuki

Based mainly on the fundamentals of *washoku*, or traditional Japanese cuisine and its emphasis on seasonal ingredients, LDH Kitchen represents the cuisine arm of LDH, with over a dozen locations in Japan. Many of the restaurants are located in the neighborhoods of Ebisu and Nakameguro, and the offerings range from soba, shabu-shabu, Japanese curry, chicken *nabemono* and *izakaya* (Japanese pub fare) to AMAZING COFFEE, a concession produced by EXILE TETSUYA. LDH Kitchen also combines LDH entertainment with food by hosting annual events such as "Izakaya EXILE PARK" (see page 200) and the recent "HiGH&LOW THE BASE," a pop-up "theme park" that ran for two months in 2016 and 2017 that served food and drink inspired by *HiGH&LOW The Movie* (see page 168).

Opposite page: Soba noodles being prepared at Nishikori, in Nakameguro, Tokyo

Above left:
The AMAZING COFFEE truck, a converted Citroën H-Type van

Above right:
Signage for the July 2014 "Izakaya EXILE PARK"

POP-UP CONCESSIONS

LDH Kitchen began with the conversion of this vintage Citroën H-Type van into the AMAZING COFFEE truck, which served beverages and snacks at a variety of EXILE events. The van and its mint-and-brown livery in turn became the inspiration for a brick-and-mortar AMAZING COFFEE shop that was erected in 2016 next to the PKCZ® Gallery Store in Nakameguro.

"Izakaya EXILE PARK" has been an LDH summer tradition for nearly a decade. Often held at one of the amusement parks on reclaimed land in Tokyo Bay, its concept and iconography is often drawn from the worlds depicted in EXILE music videos, feature films and live tours.

Arranged along a festival stage for a variety of live performances, concessions on site will invariably offer a menu designed by LDH members. Past iterations of "Izakaya EXILE PARK" have included a customized version of a particular artist or group's favorite cuisines, or else emphasizing the local specialties of a member's hometown.

CURRY SHOP
Inoue Chimpanzee
Curry – Nakameguro, Tokyo

Curry Restaurant Inoue Chimpanzee adopts the concept of "evolution" as its principal theme.

With an amazing blend of ten spices, and a subtle mildness backed up by a spicy bite, the restaurant proudly sells their own unique original curry blend. In the heart of fashionable Nakameguro, the restaurant combines the simple, satisfying pleasures of a typical Japanese curry shop and a cafe together in order to leave a lasting impression.

出雲蕎麦 錦織

NISHIKORI

Soba – Nakameguro, Tokyo

A new experience in "soba dining." Born out of Japan's Edo Period, sake and soba are embraced and enjoyed in a restaurant overlooking the Meguro River in trendy Nakameguro.

Integrating a light-filled interior made even more dramatic by cherry blossoms in the spring, LDH Kitchen, through Nishikori, strives to represent the future of "soba dining" by bringing together a refined pairing of classic soba (buckwheat noodles) with a curated selection of *nihonshu*, or traditional Japanese liquor, and specialty cocktails to create a rich dining experience.

Soba is served reflecting the traditions of Izumo (in Shimane Prefecture), which is renowned throughout Japan for noodles with a strong buckwheat flavor. Soba is freshly prepared, and served alongside other traditional dishes.

SANBAI

Izakaya - Nakameguro, Tokyo

Inside a vibrant space and an open kitchen announced by a massive live-edge wood slab counter, Sanbai provides customers with a classic *izakaya* feel, delivering expertly crafted dishes prepared and served in a warm wooden interior. *Nihonshu*, specialty cocktails and other beverages—many of which are now considered LDH standards—are enjoyed in this welcoming series of rooms, refreshing patrons in an environment that is at once familiar and novel.

鳥佳

TORIYOSHI
Yakitori – Ebisu, Tokyo

An elegant, refined yakitori restaurant in Ebisu. Upon climbing a chic little building in the heart of Ebisu customers are welcomed by the reassuring click of a traditional Japanese sliding door and the clean, minimal lines of the interior design.

To preserve the elegant simplicity of the space, only high quality *hinoki* (Japanese cypress) wood is utilized for the seats and the counters in the main and secondary rooms. The distinctive scent of the wood combines with the yakitori expertly prepared in front of the patrons, infusing the restaurant with a delicious fragrance. In addition to organic produce and specially selected ingredients, alcoholic beverages are carefully chosen to compliment and create a unique experience.

鳥雅

TORIMASA

Yakitori – Miyazaki City

Representing Miyazaki, a city and Prefecture in the southern island of Kyushu, the design of Torimasa evokes images of a green tunnel, enveloping customers in a calm and relaxing atmosphere in which patrons can enjoy their food. Upon entering, customers are seated across a modern, Japanese counter wafting with the scent of grilled chicken. Miyazaki is a region famous for its free-range *jidori* chicken, which is known for its succulent meat even under grilling, and the poultry and vegetables are all cultivated locally, matched with carefully curated liquor and other beverages.

中目黒

KIJIMA

KIJIMA

Japanese Cuisine - Nakameguro, Tokyo

With a generous view of the Meguro River, customers are invited into Kijima to escape the hustle and bustle of city life. Designed with an interior dominated by clean lines and contrasting materials, the traditional Japanese set up lends a familiar serenity, and accentuates the *washoku* expertly prepared by the kitchen. With Kijima, LDH strives to give patrons "the real thing" in both atmosphere and cuisine.

恵比寿
鳥蔵
とりぐら

TORIGURA
Yakitori – Ebisu, Tokyo

The Tokyo outpost of the famed yakitori restaurant that Hachiro Tanabe opened in Osaka in 1986, Torigura takes sure inspiration from the original.

Facing a new challenge and launching in Ebisu, Torigura encourages guests to enjoy their unique brand of chicken skewers and the chefs know just how to get it right. Originating as a cuisine for everyday people Torigura stays true to its roots while it elevates yakitori to a fine dining experience.

IEMURA

Japanese Cuisine - Ebisu, Tokyo

Taking its cues from the famed Oragamura resturant in Miyazaki City, which specializes in chicken hotpot, Iemura provides Tokyo residents the opportunity to enjoy the distinctive food of southern Japan in a modern and welcoming space.

Although comprised of a simple menu, guests are offered dishes prepared with the best ingredients, and are encouraged to return for their favorite dishes. With a menu typically only available in Oragamura, the chefs at Iemura have undergone training to create authentic regional cuisine

かとう

KATO

Kaiseki Cuisine – Ebisu, Tokyo

Chef Akihiro Kato greets all his guests and devotes himself to an attention to detail that results in a memorable culinary experience. Kato strives to create elegant, seasonal cuisine. With only ten seats available for guests, food is served in an intimate atmosphere that emphasizes the sophistication and care in which ingredients are prepared, and the supreme values that are at the heart of only the finest Japanese cuisine.

Editorial

"The main motivation behind *EXILE Magazine* was to take the group and turn it into a media platform. Although there are fan club-exclusive publications, I wasn't aware of any artists who were releasing monthly magazines with a commercial circulation in mind, and that sounded like an interesting idea, and exclusive interviews often make readers want to attend the live shows. At the beginning, the magazine featured EXILE-specific content, but now it features numerous LDH artists and has become a huge part of LDH's mentality as a progressive entertainment group."
—HIRO

EXILE MAGAZINE is an entertainment magazine published by LDH, and the first edition was released in June 2008. With HIRO as editor-in-chief, frequent editorial meetings are held to ensure diverse and exclusive content.

The magazine covers a broad range of subjects, including music, fashion, entertainment, sports, travel, and photography. Writers across the entertainment industry regularly contribute, as well as international celebrities, that in the past have included interviews with Rihanna, A$AP Rocky, Ariana Grande and Pharrell.

With many pages dedicated to members from EXILE and EXILE TRIBE, the magazine is a hit with fans. As of this writing, the periodical has a circulation of 300,000, with 100,000 regular subscribers, making it one of the more popular entertainment publications in Japan. Recently, some of the regular EXILE TRIBE segments have become so popular that spin-offs have found great success as their own releases, showing the magazine's potential to create the kind of content that appeals to a wide audience. Featured here is a selected fashion portfolio, featuring HIRO and other EXILE TRIBE members, all drawn from the last 110 issues of the magazine.

Opposite page: HIRO. Photography by Yasutomo Ebisu, 2012

Opposite and above:
AKIRA. Photography by WATARU, 2012

p.214–215:
Toshio Matsumoto. Photography by Kei Ogata, 2013

p.216–217:
Kenchi Tachibana. Photography by Go Tanabe, 2013

p.218–219:
TAKAHIRO. Photography by Taro Mizutani, 2015

p.220–221:
Naoki Kobayashi. Photography by Shiro Katagiri, 2015

p.222–223:
Ryuji Imaichi. Photography by TAKA MAYUMI, 2016

ng Area
2
Street &
icholas Avenue
r booth at other end

柿の種
100g
¥330
江戸にしき
1袋 560円
やわらか
江戸むらさき
1袋 560円
普通
江戸まき
1袋 560円
堅め
茶せんべい
1枚 65円

醤油せんべい
1枚 55円
唐辛子せんべい
1枚 65円

POLLO

Pioneer
Pioneer

p.224–225:
Alan Shirahama. Photography by Hiro Kimura, 2017

p.226–227:
Keiji Kuroki and A$AP Rocky. Photography by TAKA MAYUMI, 2015

p.228:
Hiroomi Tosaka. Photography by Kazuki Nagayama, 2016

p.229:
TETSUYA. Photography by SASU TEI, 2015

p.230:
ÜSA. Photography by Meisa Fujishiro, 2013

p.231:
MAKIDAI. Photography by TOMMY, 2011

p.232:
NESMITH. Photography by WATARU, 2011

p.233:
Sekai. Photography by Shiro Katagiri, 2017

p.234:
Hayato Komori. Photography by Rintaro Ishige, 2016

p.235:
Yuta Nakatsuka. Photography by Junji Hata, 2017

p.236–237:
Keiji Kuroki. Photography by Shiro Katagiri, 2015

p.238:
Taiki Sato. Photography by Keiichi Nitta, 2017

p.239
Mandy Sekiguchi. Photography by Toru Shiozaki, 2014

This spread:
Afrojack. Photography by Hiroyuki Matsubara, 2017

COBY

p.242:
Ryuto Kazuhara. Photography by Daisuke Mizushima, 2015

p.243:
Ryota Katayose. Photography by CHENCHE KAI, 2015

p.244–245:
SHOKICHI. Photography by TAKA MAYUMI, 2014

p.246–247:
NAOTO. Photography by Kazuki Nagayama, 2013

Previous spread:
ELLY. Photography by Motoki Mizoguchi, 2017

Above:
Pharrell Williams and ATSUSHI. Photography by Hiroyuki Matsubara, 2013

Opposite page:
Left to right: VERBAL, Pharrell Williams, and ATSUSHI. Photography by Hiroyuki Matsubara, 2013

CHANEL
CHANEL

KOMONO
PKCZ

Supreme

18

p.252–253:
PKCZ®. Photography by
Kei Ogata, 2015

p.254–255:
MAKIDAI. Photography by
HIRO KIMURA, 2013

p.256–257:
Takanori Iwata.
Photography by
Shiro Katagiri, 2016

p.258–259:
ATSUSHI. Photography by
Kei Ogata, 2015

p.260–261:
NESMITH.
Photography by
Pak Ok Sun, 2016

p.262–263:
Kenjiro Yamashita.
Photography by Tany, 2016

p.264:
ÜSA. Photography by
Itaru Chiba, 2017

p.265:
Takanori Iwata.
Photography by Tany, 2016

p.266–267:
Hiroomi Tosaka.
Photography by
Kazuki Nagayama, 2016

This spread:
Reo Sano. Photography by
Masami Sano, 2015

Following spread:
THE RAMPAGE.
Photography by
Shiro Katagiri, 2017

WORLD JAPAN ASIA EUROPE USA

apparel pictures stage music & publishing kitchen

models martial arts dance earth expg Dreams For Children

Back Endpapers:
[EXILE TRIBE
LIVE TOUR 2012
~TOWER OF WISH~]

EXILE
TRIBE